It's That Time

Jason W. Smith

The Greatest Time You Will Spend All Day

Published By:
Jasher Press & Co.
www.jasherpress.com
customerservice@jasherpress.com
1.888.220.2068

Copyright© 2015
Interior Text Design by Pamela S. Almore
Cover Design by Pamela S. Almore

ISBN: **978-0692543597**

All rights reserved. Except for brief excerpts used in reviews, no portion of this work may be reproduced or published without expressed written permission from the author or the author's agent.

First Edition
Printed and bound in the United States of America

A NOTE FROM JASON

I know that you can feel made to do a quiet time, but I want you to really take each morning, evening, or whenever the best time for you to be quiet before the Lord and hear from Him. Did you know that He really wants to speak to you and He really wants you to hear from Him? I can promise you that as you read the Word of God and ponder upon what it says, your life will be deeply challenged and impacted for the better. I know that this may be new to some of you, but it will refresh, uplift, encourage, and empower you as you begin a new day. Take seriously these devotions and begin by asking God to penetrate your heart and renew your minds with His life-giving words.

Till the Nets are full,

Jason Smith
Latitude Church
Jason@latitude.church

Table of Contents

YOU HAVE BEEN CHOSEN	9
I AM REDEEMED	11
HOW IS YOUR HEART?	13
NOW IS NOT THE TIME	15
DON'T FORGET TO PRAISE	17
YOU'VE GOT TO BE KIDDING ME!	19
IT'S NOT OVER, IT'S JUST THE BEGINNING	21
NORMAL IS SO BORING!	23
ADD SOME FRUIT TO YOUR DIET	25
WHATEVER	27
WHO'S YOUR FAVORITE?	29
WOULD YOU RATHER	31
WHERE ARE YOU RUNNING?	33
GET IN HIS SHADOW	35
MY LIFE VERSE	37
THERE'S A REASON BEHIND THE MADNESS	39
WHO DO YOU THINK YOU ARE?	41
CONSISTENCY IS THE KEY	43
ALIVE BUT DEAD	45
DEATH IS DEAD	47
NO TROUBLE AT ALL	49
A NEW REVELATION	51
WHO'S IN CHARGE HERE	53
IT WASN'T MY IDEA	55
MONKEY SEE, MONKEY DO	59
IT'S NOT A LAUGHING MATTER	61
I SAW THE LIGHT	63
FIRST THINGS FIRST	65
THEREFORE	67
I'M REALLY NOT ALL THAT	69

Day 1

YOU HAVE BEEN CHOSEN

Read: Ephesians 1:1-6

Have you ever tried out for a team or stood on the sidelines on the playground, just hoping that you would be picked next? You know that you are better than the kid who was picked before you and now you begin wandering, will I ever get picked? You finally are chosen and now it's show time! Think of this for a second, Jesus has been chosen as the captain. He is responsible for choosing His team. You are standing, with both hands raised, grunting and making noises, pick me, pick me…all of a sudden, your heart is pounding out of your chest, you feel a knot in your throat, and you are chosen for Jesus' team!

Paul tells us in these verses, "That He chose you." Jesus, the captain, the God of the universe, the creator of all things, the Great I Am, the Bread of Life, The first and the last, the bright and morning star, I could keep going! He chose you…you didn't choose Him. I know what you are mumbling, sure I did. No, He came looking for you, in your most desperate state, and chose you to be one of His children. Jesus had this planned out; He had you on His mind, as He hung on the cross. He knew that you would make a great member of His team, so He picked you. Notice how many times Paul uses the pronouns to point to Jesus. Depending on what Bible translation you have depends on the pronouns. My Bible uses about 8 pronouns referring to Jesus, just in six verses. Paul even says in verse 3, "In Christ." Everything that you will ever be, started with Christ.

WATCH WHAT JESUS DID: 1-He chose you, 2-He predestined or thought of you way before you were even born, 3-He favored you. And to think you did nothing to deserve this! Jesus chose you, you did not choose Him.

PRAY/PRAISE

Spend some time thanking and praising God for choosing you, for thinking of you way before you were born, and showing His favor on your life. Thank Him for what He has already done for you.

Day 2

I AM REDEEMED

Read: Ephesians 1:7-14

"The act of making right something that was wrong." "The payment made on behalf of another." "To compensate for the faults or bad aspects of something." These are all definitions of redemption or to be redeemed. You have heard it said that we are redeemed by the blood of the Lamb. That may sound a little churchy or you may think I am speaking Christianese! The bottom line is that we were wrong and Jesus came to make us right. We have a debt to pay and Jesus paid it in full. We are made "right" with God because Jesus redeemed us. He paid the sin debt that we owe.

Verse seven says that "we have redemption through His blood." The precious blood of Jesus forgives our every sin and makes us right with Him. Did I just rhyme? Because of the payment of Jesus' death, we are made right with God and have been given an inheritance. We have been sealed with God, not by how good we are, or how much of the Bible we know, but by what Jesus accomplished on the cross for us. Yes, for us. Everything He went through He did for you.

You are sealed with Him. This means that no one or nothing can take you out of the loving arms of Jesus. He wants you to experience His greatness and His fullness and His completeness that He gives to everyone who calls on His name.

PRAY/PRAISE

Spend some time rereading this passage. Underline, yeah it's ok to write in your Bible, the use of the word Him and He. It all rests in the finished work of Christ. You can't take any credit for this because you didn't think of it. This was His plan all along, to have a relationship with you!

Day 3

HOW IS YOUR HEART?

Read: Matthew 25:40

Being like Jesus has all to do with one's heart. When we fail to serve, love, reach, and be, we can narrow our problem down to a heart issue. The "least" of these are longing for each of us to show them the love of Christ in a real way.

Reread Matthew 25:40, seriously, reread it! Now read verses 35-36. When you begin living like Jesus, caring like Jesus, serving like Jesus, having compassion like Jesus, then are you really being Jesus. You are the hands and the feet of Jesus. We are called to show the practical love of Jesus in our daily lives. This is a practical picture of "the least of these." Now let me explain; just because some people are in extreme poverty or because they have very little to no resources, this doesn't make them any lesser to Jesus. If anything, it makes them as important as kings and queens.

The least of these represent those who Jesus came for; the hurting, the helpless, the desperate, the lost, the ones who have nothing. When we feed, clothe, provide in practical ways, then we are being like Jesus. I want to encourage you today, to continue doing what God has purposed you to do. Those who want to be first must be last. Those of us, who wish to be served, must serve. Allow your hands and your feet and your mouth and your heart to continue to point others to Christ, He may very well be all that they have!

PRAY /PRAISE

Thank God for allowing you to serve the least of these. Thank Him for providing for your health, for your finances, for your safety, and for your salvation. Ask Him to give you fresh eyes today and a fresh heart for the "least of these." Pray in expectation that the Lord will continue to use you to be Jesus in a real way.

Day 4

NOW IS NOT THE TIME

READ Galatians 6:1-10

To me, encouragement doesn't sound like this: suck it up, come on man, really, stop being lazy! Encouragement should sound like this: that a boy, great job, I knew you could do it! We all love to hear these words, especially from our teammates. We all like to be told we are doing well, but sometimes we get tired, sometimes we just don't feel like continuing to do. I want to challenge every one of us today. Find at least one person, on your team, and encourage them. Write them a note, brag about them at our group time, or simply make them feel special. I know that we can be working so hard, but feel so alone and feel like noone is noticing. I want us to be intentional in our encouragement.

Paul reminds us in what we read in Galatians, "Not to get tired of doing good." So many times we give and give with the hopes of something in return. We don't care what that something is, we just want to see or hear that something. Encouragement goes a long way and so does discouragement. What will we receive in not giving up? Paul says we will "reap" in the proper time. Reap what? Before we answer this question, let's look at how we should be responding to one another.

Verse four is the key focus for this devotion; read verse four again: "But each person should examine his own work, and then he will have a reason for boasting in him alone, and not in respect to someone else." So many times we lose our focus. Satan wants nothing less than for us to take our focus off of what our task is. He wants us to look at everyone else so as to not have to focus on us. If we look at what "ME" is doing or not doing, then "WE" will be focused on the right task. Now is not the time to point fingers, now is not the time to single anyone out, and now is not the time to get distracted from what God has called you to do. Look at you and determine if you are on task. So, what is the reward or what will we reap from doing this? What we will reap is found in verse eight: "the one who sows to the Spirit will reap eternal life from the Spirit."

Our goal is to reap an eternal harvest and to sow an abundant harvest. As you and I sow the right kinds of "seed," then we will reap the eternal inheritance of life. As we are sowing, others will see it and be drawn to it as well. Now is not the time! Keep sowing so that you can keep reaping that which is important.

PRAY/PRAISE

How have you helped carry someone's burdens? How have you gently restored another brother or sister? Are you sowing in the Spirit or in the flesh? Ask God to show you someone to help carry today. The rewards are amazing!!

Day 5

DON'T FORGET TO PRAISE

READ 1 Thessalonians 5:16-18, Psalm 86:12, Psalm 9:1

Often times we get so caught up in the daily routine of living, that we don't make time to praise God for all that He has done and is doing. If you journal, you probably have more requests than you do praises. That is really our nature, isn't it? We have needs and wants and most of the time they are legitimate. We ask God for lots of things, but do we praise Him enough for what we already have? For the next few minutes, before finishing this devotion, I want you to write down at least 10 things to praise the Lord for. Go ahead, write! OK, now let's finish. I want you to look again at your list of praises.

What do you see? Is there a pattern of your praise? I believe that the more we praise the more it excites God to keep blessing us. It's like that son or daughter who keeps asking for things, but hasn't thanked you for all that you have already done. They keep asking, we keep giving, but are they grateful for what has been done? I want you today to take time to just praise the Lord. Be open and sensitive to the Spirit and ask Him to show you things to praise Him for. Praise may be difficult for you or it may come very easy. The more you praise, the more you praise! That's smart ain't it? You may even have some Bible verses of praise that you can share with others throughout the day. Write those down and share them with someone.

PRAY/PRAISE

Praise the Lord oh my soul and all that is within me, praise His holy name! Spend time praising God that you get to have a conversation with Him, that He hears you and that He desires to hear from you. Praise God for your family, your friends, your blessings, and for using you.

Day 6

YOU'VE GOT TO BE KIDDING ME!

READ Isaiah 6:1-8

Have you ever wondered who God desires to use for His purpose and His plans? Have you ever pondered that it may very well be YOU? Uh oh!!!! I know you want to stop reading and say that this may be for pastors, teachers, missionaries, but you need to know that this is for YOU. The very first devotion we did this week talked about God choosing us and wanting us. Isaiah was no different. He was busy, he was working, he was doing what the Lord wanted him to do, but was he really? We often think by just coming to church and doing enough to "get by" that we are in the center of God's will. I may be preaching to the choir now, but Isaiah wasn't just an "attendee" he was "engaged." I know that since you are on this trip, that you consider yourself engaged. Are you really?

Engaged means that we serve, we give and we invite. We may say "I love my church" and we probably mean it. We say that we will do, we will go, we will answer the call of God, but what if that means He wants more of us? What if God says I want to stretch you a little? What if God says I want to take you out of your comfort zone? What if God says you can do more? How will you answer? We can say yes, whatever Lord, or we can say, no. There is really no in between.

I want you to consider being a sold-out, all-in, whatever it takes follower of Jesus. This may mean you have to reprioritize your life. This may mean that you have to get a little uncomfortable at times. This may mean that by being an "owner" you have to do things that you wouldn't normally do. Isaiah said, "Here am I, Lord send me." WOW!!! Send me where? Send me when? Send me to whom? Does it matter where, when or to whom? If God has chosen you, wants to use you and His will is perfect, then why not answer the same way? Lord send ME! I promise that you will not regret making this decision. You will find peace and joy in doing what God has in store for you.

PRAY/PRAISE

Ask God to show you how you can be used. What more does God want for you? How can you surrender everything to His will? Praise God that He desires for you to be all-in. It's awesome…I promise.

Day 7

IT'S NOT OVER, IT'S JUST THE BEGINNING

Well, this may have been an emotional, a tiring, a trying, and an incredible week for you. I am so thankful that you have chosen to spend time with God this week. I know your life is being transformed through getting to know Jesus. I want to encourage you to not stop. Though your journey this week has ended, your mission has not. God has been equipping you with the tools you need to serve Him. It is now that we plug in more, we dig a little deeper, we love a little wider, and we reach a little further.

It's now that we take this new fire within our bellies and let it spread to our homes, our jobs and our communities. It's now that we make the choice to either engage or attend. It's now that we invite more than ever, we give more than ever and we serve more than ever. Our fire will spread to others! God has equipped you to serve. He has gifted you to be an "owner." We have a responsibility to the Lord to try and pay back all that He has done for us. Will you accept the call of God and be willing to do, go, be whatever, whenever and however He chooses?

God is waiting on us. He is waiting on you. He is waiting on me. When we decide that we are going to be used for His glory, then He will send a revival, a fresh wind and a fresh fire over His people and those who have yet to know Him. We are the hands and feet of Jesus. How will you serve and how will you reach? It's not over, it's just the beginning.

PRAY/PRAISE

Praise the Lord for His choosing of you. Praise Him for His provision. Praise Him for the lives that you have touched. Pray that God will ignite a passion in you for the lost, for your city, for your country and for all that He is about to do in and through you!!!!

Day 8

NORMAL IS SO BORING!

READ: Galatians 5:16-21

Who likes normal anyway? I get so exhausted with hearing the same issues from people over and over. Now please understand, I am not insensitive nor have I lost that loving feeling toward people. It's just, the same song and dance over and over. Every problem is the same and every solution seems to be the same. Over the past 2,000 years, nothing has changed. What I mean is this; it's not just the lost, far from God people that are doing this "stuff." Followers of Jesus are participating in these things as well. What if I told you that Jesus was anything but normal? What if I said that Jesus was the most abnormal normal that you could ever meet? I love how abnormal Jesus is, because He is not boring.

His personality was great. He would laugh, cry, get angry, His compassion for people was huge, and He would even break up a funeral now and then. Jesus' abnormal normal is how I want to be. Notice what Paul tells us in Galatians 5:19-21. Paul knew that people were "carrying out the desires of the flesh" and he was addressing it, especially to Christ followers. Paul knew that believers in Jesus were prone to the same things as non-believers, but that believers have a new Spirit living within them. It's about to get tense!! You see, Paul knew the normal things that the "flesh" was doing. He had faced it too.

Paul knew that normal was boring and that it was time for some abnormal ways of living. For the follower of Jesus, this meant to live out, walk in, and have something different about them. Verse sixteen he says, "Walk by the

Spirit and you will not carry out the desire of the flesh." In other words, don't just say these things are of the flesh, but to walk a totally different way. This is the idea of repentance. It means to simply change the course of your life and begin living a totally different way. For the follower of Christ, this way is to be done with the "normal."

The normal fleshly desires that every human battles with, even me. These things are boring because everybody has been doing them for centuries. Why not choose to walk in the Spirit, now that's different. Read your Bible, talk about Jesus, and don't be ashamed of what He has done for you, show compassion to people, give out of abundance, and allow your life to be so different that it puts boring to shame.

PRAY/PRAISE

What about your life? Are you still living by the fleshly desires that you once had? How about thanking God for the new life, the new attitude, and the new desires you have through the Spirit filled life. Ask someone to hold you accountable to live totally different than the norm.

Day 9

ADD SOME FRUIT TO YOUR DIET

READ: Galatians 5:22-25

I want to continue this topic on living in the abnormal. If you have a mirror near you look into it. As you read this passage of Scripture, ask yourself this question; am I producing this kind of fruit? You see, you are producing fruit, no, not oranges or bananas or apples, but Spiritual fruit. Does your fruit resemble the fruit described by Paul? Some of these can be relatively easy to produce, but for some, we need some help. Are you producing this "abnormal" fruit so that others can see, taste, and experience? This is the type of fruit that the one who is filled with the Spirit of the living God will be producing. I like to say, you show me someone who is producing these fruits and I will show you someone who is maturing and growing in their relationship with Jesus.

What about you? I believe these are abnormal fruits because they cannot be produced apart from a life lived by the Spirit. You and I cannot manufacture these fruits in the flesh in which we live in. We must surrender our lives to the lordship of Christ so that we can produce a fruit that will last, be abundant, be worth producing and ultimately encourage others to produce the same. You see, the fruit the world produces, what you read yesterday, is boring, it's old, it is dead. This Spiritual fruit is alive, juicy, has a beautiful fragrance, and its taste is divine. Do you need some of this fruit in your diet? If you belong to Christ, these are not optional. God desires for us to constantly and consistently be producing this amazing fruit. How can we continue this production? Verse 16 tells us; "walk in the Spirit." We must live it out, practice these fruits daily, ask

God to help us, and watch this new fruit explode off our vines.

PRAY/PRAISE

If you are struggling with producing some of the fruit of the Spirit, ask God to search your heart. Ask God for His supernatural help. Ask Him for forgiveness from the "wrong" fruit you have been producing and ask Him to allow you to see this new spiritual fruit.

Day 10

WHATEVER

READ: James 1:2-4

Consider it a feeling of great pleasure, delight, triumph, jubilation and exhilaration when you face various trials. I can hear some of you say, "whatever." You know that word that can sometimes make you roll your eyes, turn your head and want to lay hands on someone, really hard? That word, whatever, basically says, in any circumstance. You mean when my day starts out amazing and all of a sudden I am faced with a major dilemma? You mean when I thought I was prepared for that Spanish test and just knew I would pass it and I end up failing it? You mean when my marriage is on the rocks and the verge of divorce? You mean when my child is acting like Satan's grandchild and out of control? You mean......Yes!

I mean when your world seems to be flipped wrong side up and things are completely out of your control. Whatever happens, whatever you are going through, whatever is out of your control, whatever means whatever. James exhorts those who are followers of Jesus to "consider it great joy." How could James possibly say this? You have to know who James is. He is the half brother of Jesus. This means that Jesus was not only his older brother, but James was having an identity crisis his entire life. He had to live up to Jesus, his older brother.

I can hear his parents now; why can't you be like Jesus? He made supper tonight with only five loaves and two fish. Why can't you be like Jesus? He brought Lazarus back to life. James probably struggled his entire life with thinking that he had to live up to his older brother's abilities. Now,

James is telling us to throw a party when our life gets screwed up! In every situation and circumstance that enters our lives without permission; even when that diagnosis is fatal, even when he or she decides that they don't love you anymore, even when your car won't crank for the hundredth time, consider it joy! Give God praise in the midst of the darkness. Give God praise in the midst of the storms. Give God praise when you don't feel like giving Him praise. When you and I allow our joy to overrule our circumstances, then our problems don't seem like problems. What's your "whatever" today? Consider it joy!

PRAY/PRAISE

Write out your "whatever" and speak them out loud to the Lord. He already knows them so it's ok to say them out loud. Give Him praise that He is in control of your "whatever" and ask Him to give you this same joy that James is speaking about.

Day 11

WHO'S YOUR FAVORITE?

READ: James 2:1-13

We all have favorites. I have favorite ice cream; peanut butter and chocolate from Baskin Robbins. I have favorite Bible heroes; Paul, Sampson, Peter, and especially Jesus. I have favorite tee-shirts that my wife says I wear way too much. I have favorite ball teams and favorite restaurants and favorite candy and favorite places to visit and favorite movies and favorite hunting spots, but I try not to have favorite people. Of course, my wife is my favorite and my kids are my favorite and my family is my favorite, but that's a given. I am talking about favorites as we go through life.

Growing up as a kid, we all had favorites. When it was recess and we were the captain, we picked our favorites. We picked our favorite even if they couldn't play as well as us. It's natural to pick and have favorites, but what about when it comes to seeing others through the lenses of Jesus? James talks about this in the Bible passage you just read. He calls it the sin of favoritism. What if God had favorites and you were not one of them? How would you feel? What about that person that you see almost every day. You see them at work, at school, at the park, at church, at the games, but they are not one of your favorites? They are not even close to being your favorite.

Have you ever thought that you may actually be committing a sin? That "click" you're in. That team you're on. That particular group you're in that instead of including others it isolates others. Those people or that person may actually turn out to be one of your most loyal friends you could ever have. That one person could be so desperately needing Jesus, but you are too busy or you may be concentrating on your favorites to give them the time of day. Ask God to increase your circle of influence. Ask Him to give you fresh eyes to see and a heart to reach out to someone else. Allow your favorites to be the ones that God favors.

PRAY'PRAISE

Father, forgive me when my eyes can't see any further than those I call my favorites. I want to see others as you see them; important, loved and needed. Increase my circle of influence to include those who may need you. In Jesus name.

Day 12

WOULD YOU RATHER

READ Psalm 84

We have all played this game before; Would you rather? If not, here is a little taste. Would you rather walk 3 miles barefoot or ride a bike backwards for the 3 miles? Would you rather have dirty finger nails or have them cut to the quick? Would you rather have the ability to fly or be able to run like Flash Gordon? OK, that's enough. Hopefully, you get the picture. We all have things in life that we would rather do, but for the sake of today's devotion, think about your rather with God. David says in this Psalm, "Better a day in your courts, than a thousand elsewhere." Better than a day in Hawaii? Better than a day in a tropical paradise? Better than a day at the buffet? The "courts" are referring to just the plain areas of God's presence. These places are where we probably wouldn't call an all-inclusive resort.

The places that people would look down on or not even consider wanting to hang out at. The courts represent the most insignificant, non-plush, nothing fancy place of God's dwelling. David said that he would rather hang out there than anywhere else. Anywhere else may have better accommodations, a better display of what the world has to offer, a better choice for my needs. Stop for a moment and think about this would you rather. I would rather choose a day outside of the Lord's house than a day without the Lord of the house in my life. I don't know about you, but this world has nothing for me. This world with all of its fortune and fame and prestige, has nothing I desire. I don't need any more stuff. I don't need a promotion nor a platform. I just want to be in the temple courts of my God. I want the security of knowing that I am protected, that I am cared for, that I am rescued, that I am covered, that I have a refuge and that I have a permanent home with Jesus. As the old hymn says, "I'd rather have Jesus than anything!" What about you?

PRAY/PRAISE

Think about your "would you rathers." Would you rather have the security of Christ and live in His courts or the insecurity of the world and all that it offers? Reread this Psalm and make it your anthem.
.

Day 13

WHERE ARE YOU RUNNING?

READ: Proverbs 18:10

How many times have you run away from something? If and when I ever see a snake, I run. I cannot stand snakes. If I have a feeling of fear, I run. If I am hunting and even think there may be a black bear within 100 miles of me, I run. What causes us to run? I think that we have this innate ability to run from things that frighten us. You may want to run away from that girl that is stalking you. You may want to run away from that boy who will not leave you alone. You may want to run away from that job that is sucking the life out of you. You may want to run away from some responsibilities like bills, disciplining your kids, chores, and a number of other things.

Proverbs 18:10 tells us to run to something, not away from something. The righteous run towards the name of the Lord, but often times we run away from Him. We run away because we may be afraid of what God may want for us. Notice I didn't say want from us. He wants something for us. He always has our best interest at heart and He always wants to bless his kids. That's awesome!!!!! He provides us with everything that we need, even when we think we don't need it. If you are like me, there are times where I get afraid and my instinct is to take off running away. God wants us to run to him like a scared child runs to their dad.

When we choose to run to God we are protected. If we run away from Him, it's hard for him to protect us. His name is a strong tower, a fortified city, a garrison of protection. When we make him our protector, our immediate response will be to run to him, not away. Where are you running? Do you find yourself running to Dr. Phil or to Dr. Oz for your help? Are you running to people who don't even know Jesus as their savior? If this is you, you are running to the wrong people. They are not your safety, they are not your refuge, and they are not your protector. God is your strong tower. He will not let you down. He will always provide for your protection. Those who are righteous run, but they run the right way. They run to their strong tower- God. Where are you running?

PRAY/PRAISE

Determine where you are running and then make the necessary adjustments. Some of us need to reroute our run. We need to evaluate who it is we are running to and who it is we are running from. Run to the strong tower that provides your protection.

Day 14

GET IN HIS SHADOW

READ: Psalm 91

I love to see the different shadows that different things make. As a kid, we would always try to outwit our own shadows. It was impossible until the sun went down. The verb form of the word shadow means: to follow and observe (someone) closely and typically secretly. David says, "The one who lives under the protection of the Most High dwells in the shadow of the Almighty." If you want to live under the protection and the provision of God Almighty, it's not optional for you not to follow and observe Him closely. This means that you have to stay close in your relationship with God.

You and I have to make time to be with God. We have to talk with him not at him. We have to read his word and meditate on it. We have to make appointments with him to have that alone time. We have to be intentional with how and when we are growing more in love with him. Look at your life and see if you are dwelling in His shadow. Are you protected because of where you are positioned? If you don't feel protected like you should or as close to God as you would like, look at where you are standing. Are you in His shadow? If not, you may be preventing the sun from shining through the son! It's safe in His shadow.

PRAY/PRAISE

Praise the Lord for His loving kindness. Thank Him for the shadow that he casts for you to stand under. Ask Him to allow you to see, feel and experience His shadow on a daily basis.

Day 15

MY LIFE VERSE

READ 1 John 4:1-4

For many years I was totally against tattoos. I know this may be controversial, but to me it's one of those nonessentials in the Bible. It's not worth burning this devotion or emailing me and blasting me over social media. My brothers both had tattoos and they were not hellions. They were not drug addicts nor were they criminals. They just liked tattoos. I, on the other hand, also liked them, but didn't have the money to buy one or the courage to have thousands of needles going into my flesh. When I finally convinced myself that I wanted a tattoo, I began praying about what I would get. Now, I know what you may be thinking. Here he goes justifying and making getting a tattoo a spiritual experience. No, not really. That's between me and God and you and God!

So, when I finally decided to get a tattoo, I wanted it to be a verse of Scripture that was my life verse. They say every tattoo has a story so I had to have a story if it was going to be a tattoo right? The morning I was scheduled for my tattoo, I had picked out a verse to have under my right bicep. I was certain that this verse was going to be the verse and that it was my life verse. I had rehearsed it over and over in my head and was certain this was it. As I was showering, the Lord said to me, "that's not your life verse." As I stood there with shampoo in my hair and trying to work myself up for the pain, I agreed with Him. The verse I had picked out was a great verse, but it was not my verse. Every time I would counsel someone or when I would get afraid or whenever someone needed a little encouragement, I would always quote 1 John 4:4. I was going to settle for a permanent tattoo of a verse that was not mine. I decided to get my life verse on my right arm, "Greater is He who is in me than he that is in the world." This verse has ministered to me as well as countless people I have encountered. It reassures me of who I am and whose I am. That which is inside of me gives me greater strength than the one in the world. This tattoo has been a constant reminder to me as well as those who see it. So, what's your life verse? Is it worth tattooing? Just kidding. No, is it!!

PRAY/PRAISE

Lord, help me to figuratively tattoo your Word all over me. I want to know it and know you. Thank you for the Word that transforms my life.

Day 16

THERE'S A REASON BEHIND THE MADNESS

READ: Proverbs 1:1-7

Have you ever wondered why some people do certain things or why certain things are done the way they are done? Have you ever thought about the method behind the madness? Has there ever been a time to where you just couldn't wrap your mind around why something was done that way or why that something was written? Sometimes we read passages or verses in the Bible and we find ourselves asking these questions. We stop reading and go ok, what was that written for. There is no mistake for why Solomon wrote the book of Proverbs.

In the verses you read, it spells out the purpose behind the Proverbs and actually gives you the reasons Solomon penned the words. If you have ever thought what you could get out of reading Proverbs, now you know. There are thirty one Proverbs so that means about one a day for most months. Get to reading; it will change your life!! Read the first seven verses in Proverbs chapter one again. Circle the words in your Bible that give you the purpose for the writing of Proverbs. Now do you understand why it was written? There is a reason behind the madness.

PRAY/PRAISE

Father, teach me to not just read your word, but to comprehend your word, apply your word and live by your word.

Day 17

WHO DO YOU THINK YOU ARE?

READ: 1 Peter 2:9-10

I love how Peter begins verse nine; "But YOU!" I am assuming that if you are reading this devotion that you have a relationship with Jesus, but I don't want to assume that. I know a lot of people who read the Bible, memorize the Bible, are members of a church and even give their money, but still don't have a personal relationship with Jesus. If that's you, my prayer is that after reading about who you can be in Christ, you will receive the greatest gift ever. This gift is forgiveness of your sins and freedom in your life. So, for those of us who are followers of Jesus, Peter writes these verses to you. He says that this is who you are, not who you can become. This is a present tense statement that Peter writes and is to be lived out now. This is not a futuristic promise, but a present reality.

You are: a chosen race, a royal priesthood, a holy nation, a people for His possession. If you have ever been confused about whom you are in Christ, now you know. You need to understand that you have been chosen, you have been made this nation, and you are royalty in the eyes of God. You are no longer who or what you used to be. That old way of living is gone and you are brand new. You have been made alive from the dead state of sin that you once were in and have been ushered into the marvelous light of Jesus Christ. Now that is something to get excited about! So, whenever you are asked, who do you think you are, you can reply simply with these verses. I am a chosen, royal and holy nation that once was in darkness, but now I stand in the marvelous light of His love and grace. Now that you know who you are, live like it!

PRAY/PRAISE

Thank God, for allowing you to be accepted just the way you are, but allowing you to be changed to be like Him. Spend some time praising God for who He has made you.

Day 18

CONSISTENCY IS THE KEY

READ: Ephesians 5:15-18

I love consistency, especially when it comes to where I eat. As much as I talk about food, you would think that I have a major eating disorder. I don't. I just love to eat. Anyway, there is a particular ice cream shop that my family loves to frequent at least once per week, but sometimes I get so frustrated when we go. Let me explain. I love the hand scooped ice cream, especially large scoops. I will eat soft serve, but I love large scoops of hand dipped ice cream. Did I mention large scoops of hand dipped ice cream? Just making sure. One of the things that brings out my flesh and I have to practice self-control is when I have my mind set on a particular size scoop of ice cream and I get, what I refer to as, a tick me off scoop.

This scoop is small, perfectly shaped, tiny little golf ball formed ice cream. When the person hands it to me I look at it as to say, where is the ice cream? At that moment I get in a depressed state of mind. I was thinking of the past eight times we have been and the scoops were amazing. Now, the scoop is less than desirable and it is nowhere filling to me. Consistency is the key. In life, especially as a Christ follower, we must be consistent. I don't think we should be walking around in wonder, in confusion or not knowing what is going on. We shouldn't be in sin one day and a Saint the next. Our lives should be consistent with our beliefs. Paul says to walk as wise people and not to be foolish. This means that we have some sense as believers. We ought to be living this godly life without compromise and without having to keep fighting our old nature. I know it's a battle, but we are called to be filled with the Holy

Spirit and walk according to the Spirit. Be consistent in your walk with Jesus. You may be the only consistency someone sees.

PRAY/PRAISE

In this life there will be trials and tribulations. You are called to walk wisely not foolishly. Ask God to fill you daily so that you can walk in wisdom because the world is watching. Ask Him to help you remain consistent.

Day 19

ALIVE BUT DEAD

James 2:14-26

You say you have faith, but you don't do anything about it, is it faith? You say you have works, but you don't step out in faith, is it works? There can be a lot of confusion when it comes to faith and works. Let's be clear; faith is what saves you and gives you the free gift of salvation and works is how we are justified for the free gift that we are given. I know several Christians who say they have faith, but I have never seen them put it into practice. They sit on their soft cushioned chairs and talk a great talk. When they are asked to give or to help or to serve, it's like you are asking them to give up a kidney or their first born. Their works or what I like to call their actions don't coincide with their faith. Faith and works are inseparable. They are like peanut butter and jelly, ice cream and cake, marshmallows and rice krispies, oh I can keep going! Their faith may seem alive, but their actions are lifeless.

We work out our faith in what we do for Christ. James asks the question; "what good is it my brothers, if someone says he has faith, but does not have works?" What good is saying you have this great faith, but you are not backing it up with working out your faith? James says, show me your faith and I will show you what I do with my faith. I know a lot of churches preach about having a great faith, but I think they have it all wrong. God has never called us to have a great faith. He calls us to have faith in a great God. Now that's different. Our great God can increase a little bit of our faith. Are you accompanying your faith with what you are doing for the kingdom? Some people say, you go and I will write the check. As to say, I will send my money but I won't send myself. God wants both. Don't have one without the other. Let your works demonstrate how much faith you have.

PRAY/PRAISE

Ask God to help you practice what you preach. Ask Him to give you opportunities to have your faith stretched so that it will be increased. Allow your works to coincide with what you say. Be alive in the actions of your faith.

Day 20

DEATH IS DEAD

READ: John 11:25-26

Are you the type person that stresses over death? Do you get caught up in thinking about what will happen when you die? I used to be this way until I heard a message about death being dead. It was an early, Easter sunrise service on the river when I heard this message that changed my outlook on death. It was cold, like death, and it was still dark, like death. The preacher went on with his message and I just took it all in. As he began reading about Jesus being the resurrection and the life, the sun began to rise! There began to be new life on the horizon. You could feel the warmth as if life was entering into dead bones. I began listening intently as he talked about those who are in Christ actually never dying. Never dying? I'm all ears.

Jesus was about to raise his friend Lazarus from the dead when he was confronted by two women, who were not too happy with him. After they rake Jesus over the coals, He assures them that Lazarus is just sleeping. With a dazed and confused look, they say he has been dead for four days now. We can wake up someone who is sleeping, but not someone who is dead. Jesus comforted them with who He was-the Resurrection and the life. I love how Jesus ends this fiasco and asked them a question; "Do you believe this? He says" After Jesus tells them who He is, He shows them. He raises Lazarus from the dead and he walks out of the tomb, alive and well. The same thing that happened to Lazarus will happen to those who have a relationship with Jesus. We shall never die, never! Death is dead, now that is amazing news!

PRAY/PRAISE

Thank God for the gift of life abundantly now and eternal life someday. Thank Him that we, as believers, will not have to face death, but will live forever with Him. Praise Him for that awesome gift of life.

Day 21

NO TROUBLE AT ALL

READ: John 16:33

It is a guarantee. You don't have to ask anyone about it. There is no need to fret or fear. You will have troubles in this life. You might even be thinking why am I going through what I am going through? Why do bad things seem to happen to me? What have I done to deserve this? Why can't I catch a break? The good news is God is not picking on you. He is not a cosmic kill-joy to where He will break the legs of a star quarterback and make him play the flute. God has your best interest at heart and He has greater things for you to accomplish.

When you really sit back and think about it you begin to understand that we will have troubles, but our troubles have already been overcome. We are over-comers. Jesus said, in this life you will face troubles, plural. For some of us we face more than others. So it's a guarantee that you will have problems and face troubles. It's also a guarantee that because Jesus has already overcome them, so have we. Take courage, don't be afraid, stop fretting about things because Jesus has got this. He has you and He has taken care of all of the problems you have and will have. Rest easy my friend, there's no trouble at all!

PRAY/PRAISE

Thank God for Jesus taking care of all of your problems and troubles. Rest in His care and power over every circumstance that you face. Praise Him for His awesomeness!

Day 22

A NEW REVELATION

Read: Ephesians 1:15-19

We all love new stuff. I like new shoes, new socks and new underwear. Ok, a little too much information. You like new stuff too. I know this because I see you wearing it. You can't hide it, you don't intentionally scuff up a new pair of shoes to look used, you don't rip a new shirt, and you don't break your new toy. We all like the "newness" of things. Paul speaks of a "revelation" that comes from God. Did you catch it in verse 17? Read it again. A revelation is a disclosure or an enlightening of some new truth or knowledge. Paul said that this revelation would be about the God who saved us. I have been a Christ follower for over twenty years and I am still learning new things about God. I love it! It's like getting new underwear each week!

As Christ followers, we should want and have a desire to learn something new about the God we serve. We should hunger for new revelations about Him, His character and His ways. It is time for a new revelation for our friends, our family, our communities, our schools, our city, our state, our country and our world. A new knowledge of God, not that He has changed or created anything new, but a knowledge that sets people free. Did you realize that people are not free? They are bound in sin. They are caught in the snares of life. They are broken and desperate. They are in need of a revelation from God. That He loves them, that He died for them, that He wants them, He accepts them and that He desires to be a part of their lives! You and I have seen, have tasted and have experienced this revelation Paul talks about in these verses. It's time that we go after a new revelation and spread it like wild fire. Try and learn something new about God every day. You will definitely have a "new revelation."

PRAY/PRAISE

Think about the things you know about God. Write them down. Verse 19 says that they are immeasurable. You can't put them in a jar, you cannot count them and you cannot write all of them down. They are too numerous to account for. Try today to learn something new about who God is; it's time for a new revelation!

Day 23

WHO'S IN CHARGE HERE

Read: Ephesians 1:20-23

Have you ever had a problem at a store or online trying to return or purchase something? The craziest is when you are on the phone with a business. You think and hope you have the right person, but after about a two hour conversation with them you figure they are just the janitor. How frustrating it gets when you are not talking to the person in charge.

Did you know that our churches face this dilemma all of the time? We think the pastor is in charge or the deacon board or the financial secretary. The reality is none of them are in charge! Sounds like a Harnett county boy talking- none of them! There is but one person in charge of the church. Let me break it down another way. Say you own a car, say it. I own a car. Good. Now say, just kidding, just read. This is your car, you own it, you paid for it, you clean it, you eat greasy fast food in it, you flagellate in it and you drive it. You are the owner. No one can take it away, no one can tell you what to do with it or where you can and cannot drive it.

The church is similar to your car. The church was designed by God for Jesus. It's His house. It's His bride (we will talk about that one later). We play by His rules in His house. Jesus was raised to life for the church (not the building, but the people make up the church). Christ is the head, the owner, the overseer of the church, His body. Jesus is in control. Jesus is in charge. The buck stops with Jesus. It's not your pastor, Sunday school teacher (do we even do those anymore), your choir director, your golf cart drivers, but Jesus only! If we could get that through our thick, control wanting skulls, people would run to be at church.

Paul reminds us that Jesus has been given the authority to rule over us. He is in charge. Jesus is sitting at the most respected place of authority, at the right hand of God. If someone can come back to life and be seen by over 500 people, that is who should be in charge! We are His footstool, in a good way. I will be Jesus' ottoman any day!

PRAY/PRAISE

Praise God that you are not in charge. Thank Him that He is in charge and that He is an awesome manager. Thank God for placing the "right" one at His right side. Praise God that we serve a God who is alive so that we might live!

Day 24

IT WASN'T MY IDEA

Read: Ephesians 2:1-10

Had I had anything to do with salvation, I would surely have messed it up. We all have bright ideas. Just think about Steve Jobs. He invented the I-stuff, way too many to list. Had he not had these great ideas, we would be social media poor. There would be no face time, no snap chat, no Instagram, no 4's, 5's, 5-c's, and four hundred chargers to power these things. Have you ever had a great idea and there was no way anybody else was going to take credit for it? You would go to the extreme to protect your idea. We spend millions of dollars a year just to protect our ideas with patents.

What if I told you that being alive in Christ was not your idea? What if I said that you had nothing to do with it at all? Would you argue with me? Would you prove to me that your portfolio was full of the ideas to be alive? Let's take a look at what Paul thinks about it.

First, Paul says that we were dead! Not a physical death, but a spiritual death. We were dead in our trespasses and sins. We were literally "the walking dead." Without Christ in our lives, we are considered spiritually dead living people. Think about that one. Look at verse four. I love this "but" here. Notice I didn't say "butt." That would be weird! "But God." Who? God? He had the bright idea of making us alive spiritually. You didn't, I didn't, and Steve Jobs didn't. But God did. Why would God do such a thing; great question. The answer is found in verses 4b-7. His abundant mercy not giving us what we do deserve, His great love not just any ole love, but unconditional love, His grace giving us what we don't deserve. It was God's idea to reconcile us to Himself. That's a big word that just means to be in right standing with Him. We chose to rebel against Him and He chose to rescue us out of our rebellion. Wonderful idea!

You have and never will have anything to do with your salvation. It is a free gift that cost God everything. He spared no expense to purchase your pardon. He went to the extreme to free us and save us. He gave everything so that we could receive everything. Sounds like a deal to me! You can't work for it, manufacture anything to gain it, you can't earn it and you can't be good enough for it. Salvation is based on what Jesus did, not what you and I do. Rest in knowing that somebody else's idea is greater than what you could have come up with.

PRAY/PRAISE

Praise God that you had nothing to do with salvation, that it was all His idea. Praise God for your salvation. Thank Him for giving us the ability to make the choice to choose Him. Thank Him for making you alive in Christ. Thank Him that you can stop working and trying to get to Him, because He came to you. He came to save you and to make you alive with Him!!

Day 25
THE NEW YOU

Read: Ephesians 4:22-32

Have you ever wished that you could change something, anything about yourself? You wake up and swear that you will not do what you did yesterday and as you are swearing your oath, you do it anyway? Though you have been born-again, saved, been set free, washed by the blood of the Lamb, made brand new in Christ, you and I will still struggle with this nature of ours called-sin. The good news is that you are new! You are not the same, you are not a do-over, you are not a replica, and no, God did not mess up the first time. Paul says that we are to live a new way, a new life, a new us. We can only do that through Jesus living in and through us. It is impossible to live a new you without the newness of Jesus living in us.

Living a new you requires some things from you. You must make a conscience decision, on a daily basis, yes daily, to live a new way. You show me someone who is different than the way they used to be and I will show you someone who is most likely following Jesus. When we encounter Jesus, there will definitely be a change. He doesn't make you taller or smarter, prettier or uglier. He works on the inside of you. He begins with your heart and then changes your mind.

We have to get rid or get farther away from the "old way" in which we used to live. We have to live according to the new way, God's likeness that is designed by Jesus. Paul gives some examples of how we should live. Read them and ask yourself this question; am I living this way or am I living the same way? If you are having trouble living the way Jesus says, maybe you haven't taken on this new way of living. Maybe you thought you knew Jesus, but in reality you made a decision because your friend did or your parents made you or your youth pastor persuaded you. You have to have a first-hand faith experience in order to have a new way of living.

PRAY/PRAISE

Praise God that He has given you a new life, a new way of living. Praise Him that you don't have to live the way you used to. Thank Him for His example in how to live so that you don't have to recreate the wheel. Thank Him for the "new you" and ask Him to help you with living this new way.

Day 26

MONKEY SEE, MONKEY DO

Read: Ephesians 5:1-2

Does it get on your nerves when somebody is imitating you? Do you get mad when someone buys the same shoes or outfit as you? My wife and I were driving up to a place and there were over five thousand people there. As we were looking for our group she spotted a girl with the same outfit as her. OMG!!! We almost had a melt down! My wife also had a girl her age that would buy everything the same as her. She didn't want to get anything new because she knew the moment she wore it the girl would soon have it. That can get annoying!

But what if I told you that God wants you to imitate Him? What if God said do everything as I do, live as I live, love as I love? Do you think He is annoyed with us? Not at all! He delights when we act and live like Him. Paul even says, "Imitate God." Live your life as if God is living through you. When people see you they should automatically think-God! In every area of life we should reflect the image of God. He is love, He is just and He is sacrificial.

This is how we should be. Monkey see, monkey do is a game that you basically mimic what the other person is doing. You see it, you do it. Yep, pretty boring stuff unless the person you are mimicking doesn't know you are doing it. Then it is hilarious! God wants us to imitate everything He has done and will do. This is one great way of showing others that you are living for Him.

PRAY/PRAISE

Praise God for His example; holiness, honor, sacrifice, love, acceptance. Thank Him for His constant and never changing character. Ask Him to help you imitate Him for the rest of your life.

Day 27

IT'S NOT A LAUGHING MATTER

READ: Ephesians 5:3-5

Maybe this wasn't you, but I can remember my BC (before Christ) days, when I would make harsh and rude comments to and about other people. I would hope that I would get a rise out of my friends and that they would jump in with the same sense of humor that I had. I got real down and dirty sometimes and could hang with the best of them. It wasn't until I began desiring a different way of talking and a different way of thinking and a different way of living that I realized that I was just ignorant and immature. Paul tells us in these verses that a Christ follower's lifestyle and choice of language should reflect the same as Jesus. Sexual immorality, impurities, or greed should not even be heard of among believers.

What about coarse jokes and cutting down people for the sake of a good laugh? Not even. Our entire being; our speech, our views, our living should reflect the beauty and image of Christ. How many times do we make jokes or we may even take part in laughing at them? Do you think by just laughing that we are in the clear? I think that if we are laughing and encouraging others to tell more and more jokes, that we are as guilty. Paul says, that if we partake in these things, that we will not inherit the kingdom of heaven.

I know what you are thinking; I thought the denial of Jesus as Savior and Lord was the only thing that would keep you from that inheritance. You are right. What Paul was saying was that if we are continuing to live this way after experiencing the grace, forgiveness and acceptance of

Jesus, we may need to check to see if that was for real or not. The evidence of a new life in Christ will result in new talking, new looking, new character and new living. Are you being different in your speech, are you being sexually pure and are you giving thanks for God's gift to you? If not, take a moment and ask Him to renew you, and to replace that "old" way with the new way.

PRAY/PRAISE

Father, cleanse my mouth, my eyes, my body, my spirit, my all from unrighteousness. You have given me everything to live this life in a way that will please you, so help me to continue living out this new life in Christ. In Jesus name, Amen.

Day 28

I SAW THE LIGHT

READ: Ephesians 5:6-14

It is one thing to read the Bible, pray, go to church, give your money, serve in ministry, and do it again each Sunday, but it's a totally different thing to live it. You see a lot of Christians believe that once they give their life to Jesus, they can do their own thing, live their own way, and decide their own decisions. Paul, once again, reminds us of where we came from and to where God has delivered us. "You once" is key here. Paul says, you once were in darkness. Darkness represents the ways of the world: sexual immorality, cursing, harsh jokes, name calling, lustfulness, the fulfilling of the fleshly desires, looking out for our own selfish needs and desires.

Light represents goodness, truthfulness, righteousness and joy. In the darkness of sin, we couldn't really see all that we were doing against the very God who loved us so much. In the light, our sin was revealed, it was forgiven, paid for, and we were cleansed. Paul says that it's not enough just to be in the light. It's not enough just to know that we were once in darkness and now we are in the glorious light of God's love and affection. We should be walking in the light. In our every day going, we should allow the light of God's love to shine through us. We should desire the things that are truthful, the things that are righteous, the things that are good and the things that bring Jesus joy. In doing so, others will see our light and they will be drawn closer to Christ. Are you going through the motions as a believer? Are you actually being the light? Walk out your salvation. Show others what Jesus has done for you.

PRAY/PRAISE

Lord, you delivered me out of darkness and placed me into Your glorious light. I have seen the light and now I'm asking that others would see the light in me. Help me to live out my faith in such a way, that the light of Christ would shine through me. Amen.

Day 29

FIRST THINGS FIRST

READ: Ephesians 5:18-33

I use this passage of scripture in about every wedding that I do. To me, the most important part of a wedding is talking about the one who designed marriage. I like to talk about how Jesus thinks we should be as husbands and wives, not how the world thinks we should be. You have probably read these verses before, but if you haven't, read them again, go ahead, now. OK, look at verse 18. Paul compares being filled with the Holy Spirit to being intoxicated by alcohol. What?? Paul says, "To be filled with the Holy Spirit." "Do not get drunk with wine, but." Verses 19-33 cannot possibly happen unless verse 18 is fulfilled. We must be filled with the Holy Spirit. He alone gives us strength to accomplish the tasks of being a husband or a wife.

We can't even begin fulfilling the duties and the loads of our roles until we allow God's Spirit to fill us. I have never been under the influence of alcohol. No, I am not a goody two shoes, God just spared me from having the desire to drink. I saw the effects of over indulging in alcohol and decided that I didn't need anything else to help in my overindulging. Alcohol alters our minds, alters our motor skills, alters our ability to think clearly, and it alters our decision making processes. The Holy Spirit gives us clarity, power, strength, peace, comfort and discernment. When we give control of our lives over to the Holy Spirit, then we can fulfill our duties as husbands and wives. We can only love and treat each other with the kind of love and respect that Jesus requires when we are under the influence of God's Spirit. If not, we are like someone under the effects of alcohol, and they don't have any idea what they are doing. So, when it comes to being that awesome husband and or wife, or being that awesome Christ follower, make first things first; be filled with the Holy Spirit. The only way to be filled with the Holy Spirit is to have a relationship with God through Jesus. The moment you surrendered your life to Christ, in salvation, all of the Holy Spirit made His dwelling inside of you. You have the same power that conquered death, hell and the grave, living in you. Now that's power.

PRAY/PRAISE

Father, I want to be that husband or I want to be that wife that lives according to your ways as Paul gives us in this passage of scripture. I know that in my own strength, it will not happen. I am depending on Your Spirit to fill me so that I can fulfill my role that You have called me to.

Day 30

THEREFORE

READ: Hebrews 12:1-2

Have you ever felt alone? Have you ever wondered what it must have been like to be an apostle or prophet of God? I wonder if they ever felt alone or depressed? I wonder if they pondered the thought of giving up or settling for average or just trying to fit in? I know what some of you are thinking; "They were God's chosen instruments." They were hand-picked, equipped, and God-infused for the task." Read the first word again of Hebrews chapter twelve- "Therefore." Whenever we see the word "therefore" we have to know what it is there for. Hebrews chapter eleven gives us the "therefore". This large cloud of witnesses is all of those who were justified by putting their faith into action. They didn't sit back, relax or go through the motions. They fought the good fight, they finished well.

Say this out loud; "I am not alone." Now, if you are reading this inside of Panera Bread or Chic-filet or Cookout, say it again really loud! "I am not alone." Now, if you just said that out loud, you are for sure not alone!! If security walks over to your table, just tell him about Jesus. You and I are surrounded by those who have been there, those who finished the race, those who were justified by their faithful action.

I know that it can be lonely even when we are surrounded by others. I understand that no matter how many are around us, that there are just sometimes in life that we feel like that we are on an island. Imagine how Jesus must have felt; he loved, preached, healed, made the dead alive and yet people continued to deny Him as Lord. Do you think

He felt alone at times? I think He did. But He knew that all He had to do was to remember that He was surrounded by His Father, those who loved Him and those who were reaping their rewards. So, the next time you feel alone, just remember the "great cloud of witnesses" that are cheering for you, rooting for you, encouraging you right now, to keep living for Jesus, for great is your reward.!

PRAY/PRAISE

Spend some time thanking God for His presence. Thank Him that you are not alone and that His promise is that you will never be alone. Maybe today, there is someone in your circle of influence that may think they are all alone. Text them, call them or send them a note to let them know, you are not alone!

Day 31

I'M REALLY NOT ALL THAT

READ: Ephesians 2:1-4

We make a choice everyday to either make it about us or make it about others. You probably know someone who thinks they are all that. Now don't post their name on social media! Those type people are inconsiderate of others, they look out for themselves first, and they rarely include other's opinions. It seems nearly impossible to get a word in edge wise and forget about them listening to your problems. I am certain that none of you want this to be said of you. So, you have to choose today. The Apostle Paul encouraged us to "not" to think too highly of ourselves. When we do, we don't think of others. We get so caught up in how awesome we are and all of the wonderful things we've accomplished that there is no time to think of others. Paul says, "Have the same love, same thoughts, same feelings, and to focus on the same goal." That "goal" is to put others first.

When we focus on the needs of others it helps us to do the following: 1) Do not get overwhelmed by our problems. 2) Understand and have more empathy for our neighbor. 3) Share the love of Jesus in a real and practical way. In doing so, we may actually go from a selfish person to a selfless person. Make the choice today to be about others. Think a moment with me about how Jesus thought about others. He gave His life for others. His will is that others will come to know Him. He lived a sinless life to give us an example to live by. He carried our guilt, our shame and our disgrace so that we can walk in freedom. He taught us when we were not teachable. He loved us when we were not lovable. He left the glory and splendor of heaven to come to a sinful world. He bridged the gap between us and a holy God in order for us to be forgiven, free and to reciprocate that same attitude toward others. How will you and I change the way we see ourselves so that we can see others more clearly?

PRAY/PRAISE

Spend some time thinking about how you have treated others lately. Think about how you have treated your own family, husband/wife/children. What about the people that you really love. How can you think less of yourself and think more of others? Ask God to give you the same attitude as Christ and really put others first.

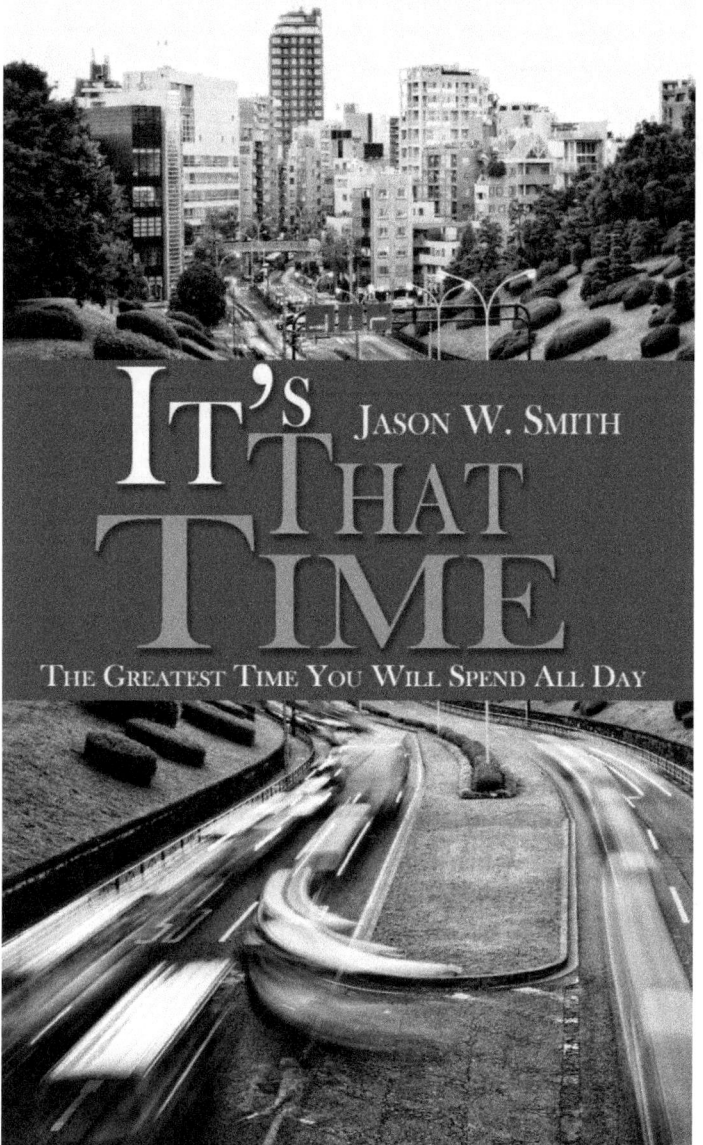

Is there a book inside of you? Ever wanted to self publish but didn't know how? Concerned about the financial part of self publishing? Relax. Take a deep breath. We can help!

Finally! An affordable Self Publishing company for all of your Self Publishing needs. We have the right services, with the right prices with the right quality. So, what are you waiting for?

Unpack those dreams, break out that pen, your dreams of getting published may not be so far off after all!

Jasher Press & Co. is here to provide you with Consulting, Book Formatting, Cover Designs, editing services but most importantly inspiration to bring your dreams to past.

And this whole process can be done in less than 90 days! You thought about it, you talked about it but now is the time!

WWW.JASHERPRESS.COM
1-888-220-2068
CUSTOMERSERVICE@JASHERPRESS.COM

www.ingramcontent.com/pod-product-compliance
Lightning Source LLC
LaVergne TN
LVHW051157080426
835508LV00021B/2671